LOVE
Psalms

Presented to:

Mom

Presented by:

Debbie

Date:

Joy Easter

LOVE Psalms

God's Gift
of Hope
and Direction

Honor Books
Tulsa, Oklahoma

Love Psalms
ISBN 1-56292-804-X

Copyright © 1999 by GRQ Ink, Inc.
381 Riverside Drive, Suite 250
Franklin, Tennessee 37064

Published by Honor Books
P.O. Box 55388
Tulsa, Oklahoma 74155

Developed by GRQ Ink, Inc.
Manuscript written by W. Terry Whalin
Cover and text designed by Richmond & Williams
Composition by John Reinhardt Book Design

*For your unfailing love
is as high as the heavens.
Your faithfulness reaches
to the clouds.*

PSALM 57:10 NLT

GOD PROTECTS HIS LOVED ONES

Shew thy marvellous lovingkindness, O thou that savest by thy right hand them which put their trust in thee from those that rise up against them.

PSALM 17:7 KJV

The single, dried rose stood alone in a small vase on the dresser, slowly collecting dust. When the flower had been fresh, it was an outward sign of a new love. But now its freshness had faded, and the dried rose exhibited a special beauty all its own. In the same way, our friends and family relationships shift and change through the years. Yet one relationship is always new. Our loving heavenly Father pours out His love on us, and our hearts bloom in His presence. Sometimes it feels as though this love fades with time, but that is only an illusion. His love for us never fails.

Whatever we face, God is with us. We can depend on His eternal love.

When I am afraid,
I will put my trust in Thee.

PSALM 56:3 NAS

Blessed are those who have
learned to acclaim you,
who walk in the light
of your presence, O LORD.

PSALM 89:15 NIV

God Loves and Helps

Help me, O Lord my God;
save me in accordance with your love.

PSALM 109:26 NIV

Sometime during their marriage, the Harolds stopped talking about anything important. It worried Cindy, but Bill didn't seem to notice. Cindy decided their relationship needed nurturing to grow, so, despite her trepidation, she initiated a dialogue about her real feelings. Because he was just as committed to their marriage, Bill responded by sharing more of himself—emotionally, verbally, and spiritually. Their love for each other deepened because they were no longer just dealing with their external circumstances, but rather were communicating heart to heart.

Our heavenly Father also wants an intimate relationship with us, but we must nurture His love with time and prayer. Draw near to God, and He will draw near to you.

Our soul waits for the LORD;
He is our help and our shield.

PSALM 33:20 NAS

Come quickly! Help me, O my Savior.

PSALM 38:22 TLB

God is our refuge and strength,
a very present help in trouble.

PSALM 46:1 NRSV

Trust in God's Unfailing Love

I trust in your love.
My heart is happy
because you saved me.

Psalm 13:5 NCV

❧

As Carol maneuvered through traffic on her way to work, she thanked God for all the wonderful things He had done for her. She had a new job, a great husband, and two terrific children. Distracted, she failed to notice the red light until she reached the intersection. Carol slammed on her brakes. Thankfully, they worked, and she avoided a collision. As she waited for the light to turn green, she realized how many things she and her friends take for granted: brakes that work, safe neighborhoods, and loving families.

Instead of taking our family and friends for granted, we should nurture their feelings of trust, respect, and love. And just as we nourish others, it is even more important to spend time with God, loving Him through prayer and studying Scripture. When we trust in His love for us, our hearts overflow like streams of living water.

Light shines on the godly, and joy on those who do right.
May all who are godly be happy in the Lord
and praise his holy name!

Psalm 97:11–12 nlt

No wonder we are happy in the Lord! For we are trusting him.
We trust his holy name.
Yes, Lord, let your constant love surround us,
for our hopes are in you alone.

Psalm 33:21–22 tlb

THINK ABOUT GOD'S LOVE CONSTANTLY

Oh, how I love your law!
I think about it all day long.

PSALM 119:97 NLT

Our time is limited. Each of us only has twenty-four hours a day to spend, and no matter what we do, it can't be multiplied. Staying up late and getting up early is not the answer. Eventually, we burn out, and life seems like drudgery. Yet for couples or long-term friends to develop stronger, healthier relationships, spending time with them is essential. The most precious gift you have to give is the hours in the day you spend with them. We all need attention.

In the same way, we strengthen our love for the Lord of the universe by spending time with Him, listening to His still, small voice.

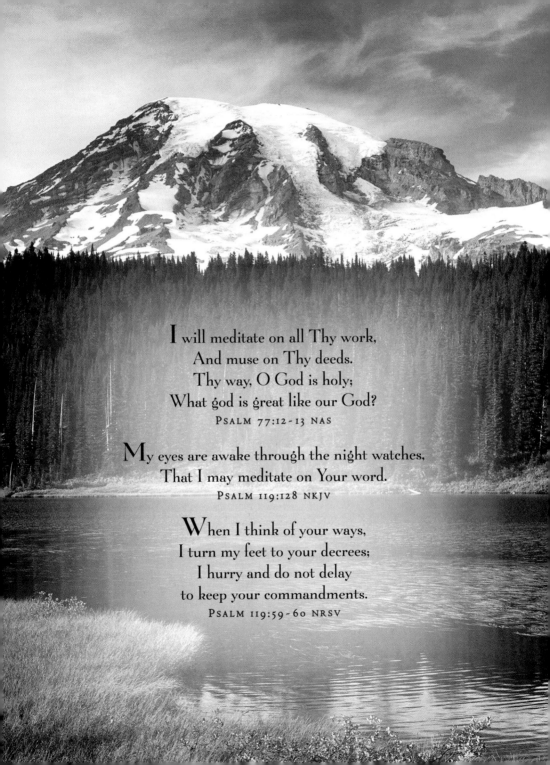

I will meditate on all Thy work,
And muse on Thy deeds.
Thy way, O God is holy;
What god is great like our God?

PSALM 77:12-13 NAS

My eyes are awake through the night watches,
That I may meditate on Your word.

PSALM 119:128 NKJV

When I think of your ways,
I turn my feet to your decrees;
I hurry and do not delay
to keep your commandments.

PSALM 119:59-60 NRSV

Love Keeps Us Safe

Praise be to the LORD,
for he showed his wonderful love to me
when I was in a besieged city.

Psalm 31:21 NIV

A s she puttered in the yard, Nancy remembered her neighbor's stinging words, "Why don't you fix your back fence before it falls down?" One moment, life was full of joy, and in the next, she could no longer enjoy the song of a robin on the fence post. We all go through tests of our patience. Like the old walled cities, frequently surrounded by enemies, maybe you feel besieged right now.

Take heart! Even in the midst of the enemy, God blesses us with His wonderful love and presence.

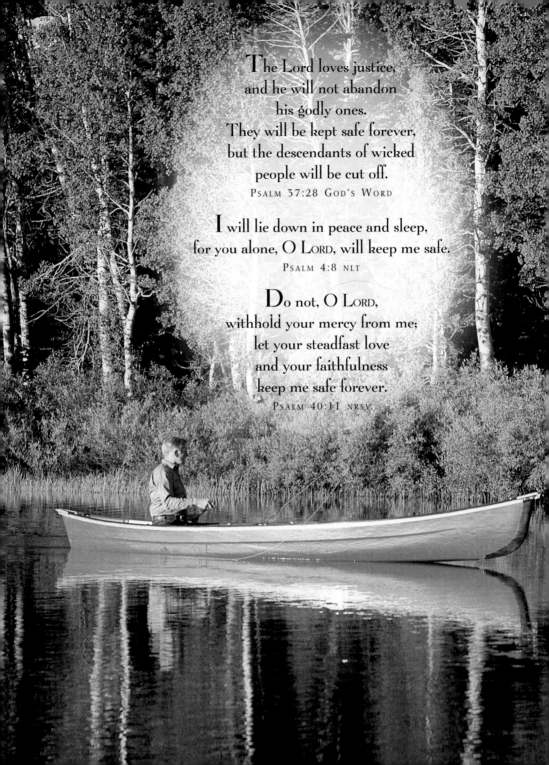

The Lord loves justice,
and he will not abandon
his godly ones.
They will be kept safe forever,
but the descendants of wicked
people will be cut off.

PSALM 37:28 GOD'S WORD

I will lie down in peace and sleep,
for you alone, O LORD, will keep me safe.

PSALM 4:8 NLT

Do not, O LORD,
withhold your mercy from me;
let your steadfast love
and your faithfulness
keep me safe forever.

PSALM 40:11 NRSV

GOD'S LOVE IS MERCIFUL

Do not remember the sins of my youth
or my rebellious ways.
Remember me, O Lord, in keeping with
your mercy and your goodness.

PSALM 25:7 GOD'S WORD

Almost everyone lives with some measure of regret. Maybe for you it's as fresh as a harsh word you spoke a few hours ago. You didn't mean to blurt out those words that hurt your best friend. Or possibly you regret rebelling against your parents when you were a teenager. You continue to carry the pain and sadness of their disappointment. Maybe you are grieving for a missed opportunity. Thankfully, we don't have to allow regrets to torment us.

Talk to God about your regrets and allow Him to heal the pain of your past and fill your life with His goodness and mercy.

But Thou, O Lord, art a
God merciful and gracious,
Slow to anger and abundant
in lovingkindness and truth.

PSALM 86:15 NAS

But I have trusted in Your mercy;
My heart shall rejoice in Your salvation.

PSALM 13:5 NKJV

Help us, O God of our salvation,
for the glory of your name;
deliver us, and forgive our sins,
for your name's sake.

PSALM 79:9 NRSV

THE LOVE OF GOD SURROUNDS US

Lord, I love your home,
this shrine where the brilliant,
dazzling splendor of your presence lives.

PSALM 26:8 TLB

Catherine's heart swelled with love as she watched her daughter, Tracy, receive her high school diploma. Tracy's generous nature and ready smile had endeared her to everyone, including the young people at the sheltered workshop where she volunteered. Tracy possessed something precious. God had made His home in her heart.

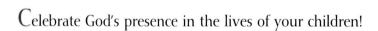

Celebrate God's presence in the lives of your children!

As the mountains surround Jerusalem,
the LORD surrounds his people
now and forever.

PSALM 125:2 NCV

Every path of the Lord is one of mercy and truth
for those who cling to his promise
and written instructions.

PSALM 25:10 GOD'S WORD

Surely goodness and lovingkindness will
follow me all the days of my life,
And I will dwell in the house of the LORD forever.

PSALM 23:6 NAS

Because Your lovingkindness is better than life,
My lips shall praise You.

PSALM 63:3 NKJV

God's Love Is Precious

How precious is Your lovingkindness, O God! Therefore the children of men put their trust under the shadow of Your wings.

PSALM 36:7 NKJV

As Daniel rummaged through a bedroom drawer, he stumbled across a letter written by his mother five years earlier. The envelope had faded to a pale pink, and her handwriting was shaky where she had written his address. Inside was a single sheet of paper. His mom loved frilly stationery with lacy edges. Daniel reread where she thanked him for his time and the family's visit; then some words leaped off of the page as they had many times before: "I'm so proud of you and your family and how your life has turned out."

God has written us a personal letter—the Bible—that is far more valuable, encouraging, and life changing than any note delivered by the postal service. We can read it over and over, but it's always new.

How precious are your thoughts about me, O God!
They are innumerable!
PSALM 139:17 NLT

The LORD is just in all his ways, and kind in all his doings.
PSALM 145:17 NRSV

He will save them from oppression
and from violence, for their lives are precious to him.
PSALM 72:14 TLB

Let the kindness of the Lord our God be with us.
Make us successful in everything we do.
Yes, make us successful in everything we do.
PSALM 90:17 GOD'S WORD

LOVE OF GOD BRINGS STRENGTH

I will love You, O LORD, my strength.

PSALM 18:1 NKJV

❧

Sally smiled at her husband as he easily lifted the box of books from the trunk of her car. When she had first met John, she had been overwhelmed by his towering strength, but now she only felt safe and secure with him. John had learned a key lesson about love. Instead of using his strength to dominate their relationship, he constantly searched for new ways to love and enrich her.

It's the same in our relationship with God. He spoke the world into existence with great creativity and strength, yet He cares for us in the most tender ways. The same God who created the power of thunder and lightning also crafted the most delicate violet. Thank the Lord for both His love and strength.

He gives me new strength.
He leads me on paths that are right
for the good of his name.
PSALM 23:5 NCV

On God my salvation and my glory rest;
The rock of my strength,
my refuge is in God.
PSALM 62:7 NAS

My life is an example to many,
because you have been my
strength and protection.
PSALM 71:7 NLT

GOD'S LOVE FILLS OUR HEARTS WITH SONGS

*Through each day the LORD pours his
unfailing love upon me,
and through each night I sing his songs,
praying to God who gives me life.*

PSALM 42:8 NLT

In Rosemary's search for a new job, doors seemed to slam in her face. She continued to look, yet for each position, her skills didn't quite measure up. Undaunted, she continued to search with anticipation and hope. Her friends marveled at her unfailing trust in God. Rosemary had learned there were only two basic responses to every situation in life. One says, "How terrible," and the other says, "Things can only get better!"

We need to cast ourselves into God's capable hands and depend on His love. He is the One who fills our lives with music. Difficulties need not break us; they can increase our love for life and bring us closer to God.

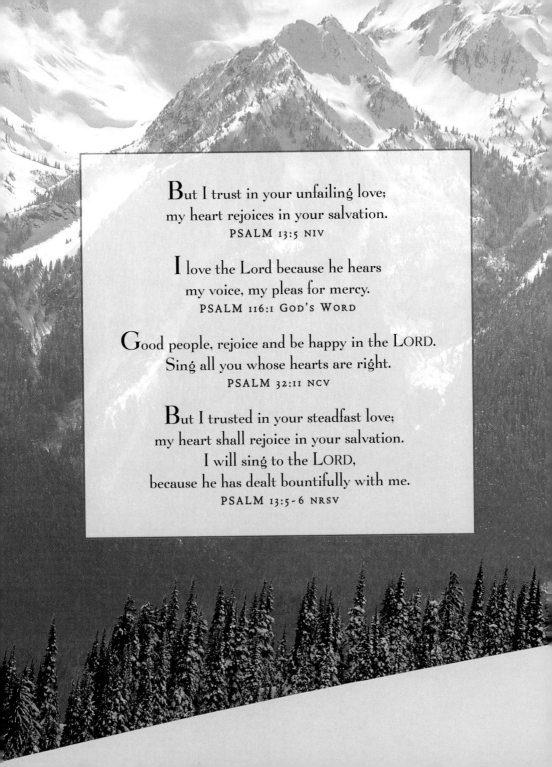

But I trust in your unfailing love;
my heart rejoices in your salvation.
PSALM 13:5 NIV

I love the Lord because he hears
my voice, my pleas for mercy.
PSALM 116:1 GOD'S WORD

Good people, rejoice and be happy in the LORD.
Sing all you whose hearts are right.
PSALM 32:11 NCV

But I trusted in your steadfast love;
my heart shall rejoice in your salvation.
I will sing to the LORD,
because he has dealt bountifully with me.
PSALM 13:5-6 NRSV

LOVE IS WONDERFUL

*My strong love for your Temple
completely controls me.
When people insult you, it hurts me.*

PSALM 69:9 NCV

During his teen years, Kyle had been teased by some of his friends for spending Sunday mornings and Wednesday nights at church. He could never stay out past midnight on a Saturday night. At the time, he resented his parents for their strict adherence to saying a blessing over their food–even in public. Now that he is a father himself, he understands. He is so thankful his parents have passed on their love of God to him, just as he will teach his children to love the Lord.

True to His Word, God will control our lives with love when we turn to Him. His heart is always open and waiting.

I will talk to others all day long
about your justice and your goodness.
For all who tried to hurt me have been
disgraced and dishonored.

PSALM 71:24 TLB

I have become an example to many people,
but you are my strong refuge.

PSALM 71:7 GOD'S WORD

For You have been a shelter for me,
A strong tower from the enemy.

PSALM 61:3 NKJV

GOD'S LOVE IS TESTED AND PROVEN

Your promises have been thoroughly tested;
that is why I love them so much.

PSALM 119:140 NLT

Rebecca smiled in delight as she discovered the small diamond ring inside her mother's antique jewelry box. As a

child, she remembered her mother always wore the ring, even when mopping floors or doing dishes. But after the premature death of Rebecca's father, the ring disappeared from her mother's finger. Now her elderly mother had joined her beloved husband in heaven. The ring brought back the promises her mother had taught her as a little girl. Marriage is a covenant, and the ring signifies the joining of two hearts.

Since the beginning of time, families have tested God's promises and found them to be steadfast and true—just like a well-worn ring.

Thou hast tried my heart;
Thou hast visited me by night;
Thou hast tested me and dost find nothing;
I have purposed that my mouth will not transgress.

PSALM 17:3 NAS

The promises of the LORD are
promises that are pure,
silver refined in a furnace on the ground,
purified seven times.

PSALM 12:6 NRSV

For You, O God, have tested us;
You have refined us as silver is refined.

PSALM 66:10 NKJV

I am trusting God—oh, praise his
promises! I am not afraid of anything
mere man can do to me! Yes, praise his promises.

PSALM 56:10-11 TLB

Your kingdom is an everlasting kingdom,
and your dominion endures through all generations.
The LORD is faithful to all his promises
and loving toward all he has made.

PSALM 145:13 NIV

GOD'S LOVE IS FOREVER

For I have said, "Lovingkindness
will be built up forever;
In the heavens Thou will
establish Thy faithfulness."

PSALM 89:2 NAS

Every morning, Robert woke his wife with a gentle touch and a tender kiss. Since the day after their wedding some twenty years ago, he had faithfully fulfilled his promise to love and cherish her. In his loving gestures, he wanted to build up his wife for the day ahead. Not everyone would treat her with respect, and there would be those who would be rude and unkind. But she would always know that his love would be waiting at the end of the day.

God is faithful to His promises; His love for us is eternal and unchanging.

Your kingdom is an everlasting kingdom,
and your dominion endures
through all generations.
The LORD is faithful to all his promises
and loving toward all he has made.

PSALM 145:13 NIV

But know that the LORD has set
apart the faithful for himself;
the LORD hears when I call to him.

PSALM 4:3 NRSV

Let me live in your Holy Tent forever.
Let me find safety in the shelter of your wings.

PSALM 61:4 NCV

LOVE TRIUMPHS OVER EVIL

But I will sing of your might;
I will sing aloud of your
steadfast love in the morning.
For you have been a fortress for me
and a refuge in the day of my distress.

PSALM 59:16 NRSV

Not a leaf stirred in the hot, still afternoon as a dark, ominous cloud rolled over the horizon. Jesse and Shirley herded their children into the basement to await the storm that was sure to come. They didn't need to hear the warnings on the radio. They had lived through so many tornado alerts, they knew all the danger signs. In the gathering darkness, Shirley led their four children in singing songs of praise to God, passing on her trust in His sure protection. While the wind howled and the thunder rumbled, they nestled safe in God's hands.

The Lord constantly reminds us that He gives us refuge from life's storms. He is our fortress. Every morning, let's sing the praises of the Lord our God.

I will give thanks to the LORD
according to His righteousness,
And will sing praise to the
name of the LORD Most High.

PSALM 7:17 NAS

My heart is steadfast, O God,
my heart is steadfast;
I will sing and make music.

PSALM 57:7 NIV

Sing a new song to the Lord!
Sing it everywhere around the world!

PSALM 96:1 TLB

GOD'S LOVE RESCUES US

For the Lord says, "Because he loves me,
I will rescue him; I will make him great
because he trusts in my name."

PSALM 9:14 TLB

Stage fright.
Stephanie's heart pound-
ed in her ears as she
stood before the class to
deliver her first speech,
fearing she would make
a fool of herself. She
cleared her dry throat
and tried to hold steady
her page of notes. Her
writing seemed like
gibberish. Then a Bible verse she had memorized in Sunday
school drifted into her paralyzed mind: *I can do all things
through Christ who strengthens me.* She took a deep breath and
plunged ahead, trusting God to help her.

Cry out to God today, and He will rescue you because of His
great love. Trust in Him, and He will give you the desires of
your heart.

I come to you for protection, O LORD my God.
Save me from my persecutors—rescue me!
PSALM 7:1 NLT

Turn your ear to me,
come quickly to my rescue;
be my rock of refuge,
a strong fortress to save me.
PSALM 31:2 NIV

Happy is the person who trusts the LORD,
who doesn't turn to those who are proud
or to those who worship false gods.
PSALM 40:4 NCV

Protect me, because I am faithful to you.
Save your servant who trusts you.
You are my God.
PSALM 86:2 GOD'S WORD

Love Comforts Us

*Let, I pray thee, thy merciful kindness
be for my comfort, according to thy
word unto thy servant.*

PSALM 119:76 KJV

Little girls stub their toes, and small boys scrape their knees. Children fall down and cry; moms and dads kiss tear-wet cheeks and smooth back damp curls. Hugs make the pain go away. Then we grow up. Daddy isn't there to fight our battles, and Mama's lap is out of reach. But we can call on our heavenly Father, who is always waiting for our whispered prayer, and He will lift us up into His loving arms.

God's mercy is always reaching out to us–even when we temporarily fall out of fellowship with Him. If we will only turn our eyes to Him, His love will fill and comfort our lives.

You will increase my honor
and comfort me once again.
PSALM 71:21 NIV

But you, O Lord, are a compassionate
and merciful God.
You are patient, always faithful and
ready to forgive.
PSALM 86:15 GOD'S WORD

The LORD is merciful and gracious;
he is slow to get angry and full of unfailing love.
PSALM 103:8 NLT

LOVE'S CONNECTION TO JOY

I will rejoice and be glad
in Thy lovingkindness,
Because Thou hast seen my affliction;
Thou hast known the troubles of my soul.

PSALM 31:7 NAS

Vicky's whole day had been like one that daily tests and tries men's souls. Jangling phones . . . a burger on the run . . . traffic jams. And now this. Her blurred vision was the only warning of the splitting migraine before it pierced her right temple with heat-seeking missiles of pain. Fumbling for the medication in her purse, she pulled into a convenience store lot, closed her eyes, and laid her head on the steering wheel. She cried out to God in prayer, "Lord, help me!" A quiet voice immediately spoke to her heart, *I will never leave you nor forsake you.* Even in the midst of pain, her heavenly Father was with her, and she thanked God for His ever-present love.

With understanding of God's love and concern for us, we can experience and praise Him, even when we are ill or in trouble.

You have seen me tossing and turning through the night. You have collected all my tears and preserved them in your bottle! You have recorded every one in your book.

PSALM 56:8 TLB

He has remembered his love
and his faithfulness
to the house of Israel;
all the ends of the earth
have seen the salvation
of our God.

PSALM 98:3 NIV

For He has delivered me out of all trouble;
And my eye has seen its desire upon my enemies.

PSALM 54:7 NKJV

GOD'S FAITHFUL LOVE

*[The Lord of lords] brought Israel out from among them,
for his steadfast love endures forever.*

PSALM 136:11 NRSV

The church bell sounded, and memories of the past flooded his heart. It was forty years ago that Deborah and he walked out of the church to the sound of those bells on their wedding day. Yet it only seemed like yesterday. That first year, romance was soon replaced by reality–baby beds, midnight croup, and monthly bills. Now her silvered head leaned on his shoulder in the bright sunshine. He squeezed her arm and helped her down the stairs. She was his best friend. With each passing year, his love for her deepened and matured. They were as comfortable as old slippers, and yet each day he fell more in love with her. The bell reminded him of their faithfulness to one another.

Our relationship with God is constantly growing. At first, we are stirred with His amazing love. Then through the years, we stand amazed at the Lord's consistent and enduring love. Today, let's celebrate God's faithful love.

For he loves us with unfailing love;
the faithfulness of the LORD
endures forever.
Praise the LORD!

PSALM 117:2 NLT

Thy kingdom is an everlasting kingdom,
And Thy dominion endures
throughout all generations.

PSALM 145:13 NAS

Respect for the LORD is good;
it will last forever.
The judgments of the LORD are true;
they are completely right.

PSALM 19:9 NCV

LOVE HONORS OTHERS

LORD, you do everything for me.
LORD, your love continues forever.
Do not leave us, whom you made.

PSALM 138:8 NCV

During the long days of winter, Della had longed for and anticipated the first green shoots in her garden. Now they were standing tall in the moist, black soil. After the dark clouds rolled over the horizon and a gentle rain soaked the earth, the crocus buds quickly swelled. By Sunday morning, a yellow mass of flowers filled the beds. She rejoiced at the signs and smells of new life and the reminder of God's faithful love. Even when she couldn't see life in the dead, cold ground, His seeds were preparing to spring forth in a symphony of color.

In the same way, God is working inside our hearts, whether we're aware of it or not, preparing us for loving fellowship with Him.

He who forms the hearts of all,
who considers everything they do.

PSALM 33:15 NIV

Surely goodness and lovingkindness will
follow me all the days of my life,
And I will dwell in the
house of the LORD forever.

PSALM 23:6 NAS

THE LOVE OF GOD SURROUNDS US

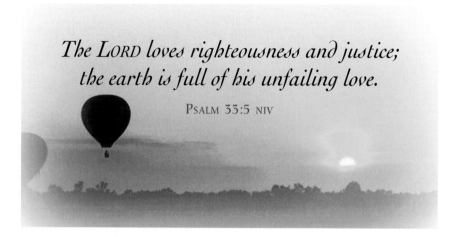

*The LORD loves righteousness and justice;
the earth is full of his unfailing love.*

PSALM 33:5 NIV

Carolyn, falsely accused of lying about completing an assignment, stood before her manager, defending herself against the allegations. "I put the report in your box, Mr. Dale," she said. "Then where is it?" he yelled, scrambling through the stacks of paper on his desk. "It's due on Carter's desk in ten minutes!" Rather than lose her temper, Carolyn calmly searched through his in-basket and then the trash basket next to his desk. Just as she suspected, part of the tall stack had slipped into the waste can. As she handed him the report, she smiled sweetly before walking back to her office, confident in God's love for her.

When we face injustice, we can always celebrate God's gentle and unfailing love for us. Today, let Him rescue you from an uncomfortable situation.

The Lord loves justice,
and he will not abandon his godly ones.
They will be kept safe forever,
but the descendants of wicked people
will be cut off.

PSALM 37:28 GOD'S WORD

Surely goodness and mercy shall follow me
All the days of my life;
And I will dwell in the house of the LORD
Forever.

PSALM 23:6 NKJV

Pour out your unfailing love on
those who know you! Never stop
giving your salvation to those who
long to do your will.

PSALM 36:10 TLB

All the paths of the LORD are
steadfast love and faithfulness,
for those who keep his covenant
and his decrees.

PSALM 25:10 NRSV

LOVE REVEALS GOD'S PLAN

*The Lord will work out his plans
for my life—for your lovingkindness,
Lord, continues forever. Don't
abandon me—for you made me.*

PSALM 138:8 TLB

Jim's business was failing. He had done everything he knew to do; he had talked to his bankers and staved off foreclosure. But each day he hurtled toward the cliff of bankruptcy. Defeated, he knelt beside his chair to pray. Only a miracle would save him from his creditors. As he asked God for His perfect plan, Jim realized where he had gone wrong. Instead of putting God first in his life, he had put Him last . . . right behind his own family. He realized he was in danger of losing his business, but more important, he was in danger of losing his wife, his children, and his faith. It was time to set his priorities straight, and he prayed that God would show him how.

God has designed a long-range plan for our lives in His lovingkindness. If we follow his blueprint for success, He will help us build our dreams and reach the goals He has placed in our hearts.

O LORD my God, you have done many
miracles for us.
Your plans for us are too numerous to list.
If I tried to recite all your wonderful deeds,
I would never come to the end of them.

PSALM 40:5 NLT

GOD'S LOVE NEVER FAILS

*Forgive the rebellious sins of my youth;
look instead through the eyes of your
unfailing love,
for you are merciful, O LORD.*

PSALM 25:7 NLT

When Karen thought about her college years, she cringed in embarrassment. In rebellion, she had plunged into a wild lifestyle that seemed to haunt her adult years. The friends she associated with now in her new job didn't know about her past. She was engaged to a wonderful man who thought she was sweet and innocent. It was a fresh start, yet she wondered if she could find forgiveness for the rebellious activities of her youth.

No matter what we've done in the past, God has a vast amount of mercy to pour into our situation. Through the power of His Spirit, God can heal any pain from our past. Let's celebrate the vast forgiveness and mercy of God's love!

For You, Lord, are good, and
ready to forgive,
And abundant in mercy to all
those who call upon You.

PSALM 86:5 NKJV

But there is forgiveness with Thee,
That Thou mayest be feared.

PSALM 130:4 NAS

God Never Abandons Us

In your unfailing love, silence my enemies;
destroy all my foes,
for I am your servant.

PSALM 143:12 NIV

From her first days on the job, Jenny felt as though she had talked herself into a position that was far beyond her skill level. She constantly made mistakes, and the more she worried, the more she seemed to fail and the more her coworkers expressed frustration at her performance. Then her supervisor called her in. "I have faith in you, Jenny, and I know you can improve your effectiveness. Have you considered taking a few refresher courses?" Instead of feeling condemned, Jenny was encouraged to go back to school, and her skills steadily improved.

Sometimes, we are our own worst enemy, but we can find a fresh source of strength and power from our heavenly Father. Move into His presence and let His enduring love give you peace.

Pour out your unfailing love on those
who know you! Never stop giving your
salvation to those who long to do your will.
PSALM 36:10 TLB

All the paths of the LORD are
steadfast love and faithfulness,
for those who keep his covenant
and his decrees.
PSALM 25:10 NRSV

THE LOVE OF GOD BRINGS VICTORY

*Great triumphs he gives to his king,
and shows steadfast love to his anointed,
to David and his descendants forever.*

PSALM 18:50 NRSV

One day while searching in the attic, Sarah found an old trunk. She shoved open its heavy lid and, among the old clothing, discovered a leather-bound Bible. Inside its yellowed pages, Sarah found a brief record of her family history. She had grown up as an only child. Her parents rarely discussed the family history. Now they were both gone, and she had no one to ask. Inside the worn Bible, Sarah found an unexpected treasure of her past—notes about her grandparents and great-grandparents, including their occupations and birth and death information. But more important, she found the record of God's steadfast love throughout history and His plan of salvation through His Son, Jesus Christ.

No matter what man has done, God has continued to reach out with His love. He's still reaching out to us today.

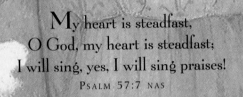

My heart is steadfast,
O God, my heart is steadfast;
I will sing, yes, I will sing praises!

PSALM 57:7 NAS

Sing to the LORD a new song,
because he has done miracles.
By his right hand and holy arm
he has won the victory.

PSALM 98:1 NCV

Show me your unfailing love in wonderful ways.
You save with your strength
those who seek refuge from their enemies.

PSALM 17:7 NLT

GOD'S LOVE IS KIND

*The Lord taketh pleasure in them that
fear him, in those that hope in his mercy.*

PSALM 147:11 KJV

❧

"Did Billy's cat go to heaven?" three-year-old Shane asked his mother. It was a simple child's question. "Well, honey," she said slowly, "we know God loves kitty cats, and He made them for us to enjoy. What do you think?" "I think God has kitties," he said. "I'm sure He does," she said. Sometimes, Shane's mother didn't have all the answers for her son, and as he grew older, there would be even tougher challenges to face. *Why did Grandpa die? Why did my teacher move away? Why can't I stay out past midnight?* In the swirl of change, we can turn to the source that never changes–the eternal God.

His mercies are new every morning and carry great hope for our future.

LORD, don't hold back your
tender mercies from me.
My only hope is in your unfailing love
and faithfulness.

PSALM 40:11 NLT

So, Lord, what hope do I have?
You are my hope.

PSALM 39:7 NCV

The Lord advises those who fear him.
He reveals to them
the intent of his promise.

PSALM 25:14 GOD'S WORD

Never-Ending Love
Surrounds the Faithful

Many sorrows come to the wicked, but abiding love surrounds those who trust in the Lord.

PSALM 32:10 TLB

On the morning of their twenty-fifth anniversary, Mark surprised his wife with a single diamond on a simple gold chain. As he fas-tened it around her neck, she reached up and touched it gently. "This is for all the diamonds you sacrificed so we could buy school clothes and replace kitchen faucets," he said lovingly. "Happy anniversary, darling." She would always treasure the necklace as a reminder of her husband's love.

As we move through our day, we have no visual picture of God, yet we feel His love surrounding us. It fills our hearts and days with His never-ending, life-enhancing presence.

But I trust in your unfailing love.
I will rejoice because you have rescued me.
PSALM 13:5 NLT

Some trust in chariots, and some
in horses: but we will remember
the name of the LORD our God.
PSALM 20:7 KJV

Even when I am afraid, I still trust you.
PSALM 56:3 GOD'S WORD

Trust in the LORD and do good;
so you will live in the land, and enjoy security.
PSALM 37:3 NRSV

GOD'S DELIGHT
IS THOSE WHO HONOR HIM

*Every path of the Lord is one
of mercy and truth
for those who cling to his promise
and written instructions.*

PSALM 25:10 GOD'S WORD

E roded by the winter rains, the path down to the beach was treacherous in places. But Carla had been cooped up in the house for a week, and now the sun was warm on her face. She looked down at the rocks below and hesitated. Then tucking her leather book under one arm, she clung to a deeply rooted bush and slid the rest of the way down. Freedom at last! She breathed deeply of the fresh, salty air, then found a nesting place between the rocks. Opening her Bible, she began to read, "In the beginning, God created. . . ."

We can honor God as we delight in His promises and written instructions.

But I have trusted in thy mercy;
my heart shall rejoice in thy salvation.
PSALM 13:5 KJV

He will keep his agreement forever;
he will keep his promises always.
PSALM 105:8 NCV

Open my eyes, that I may behold
Wonderful things from Thy law.
PSALM 119:18 NAS

They fill their hearts with God's law,
so they will never slip from his path.
PSALM 37:31 NLT

Make me walk in the path of
Your commandments,
For I delight in it.
PSALM 119:35 NKJV

Wisdom Is Following God's Love

Whoever is wise, let him heed these things and consider the great love of the Lord.

PSALM 107:43 NIV

Our lives are filled with choices. We worry: What if I choose the wrong mate and our marriage ends in divorce? What if I eat too much over the holidays and gain weight? What if I choose

the wrong career and I'm bored the rest of my life? We don't have to worry. God allows course corrections!

In large and small decisions, we can ask for help and receive it from the Lord of the universe. God cares about the paths we choose. Ask for His wisdom and love as you make the choices of today.

Yet, you desire truth and sincerity.
Deep down inside me you teach me wisdom.

PSALM 51:6 GOD'S WORD

So teach us to number our days,
That we may gain a heart of wisdom.

PSALM 90:12 NKJV

The LORD says, "I will make you wise
and show you where to go.
I will guide you and watch over you."

PSALM 32:8 NCV

God's Love Keeps Us from Stumbling

For the king trusts in the LORD.
The unfailing love of the Most High will
keep him from stumbling.

PSALM 21:7 NLT

Whee," the little boy cried out as his mother held his arms and twirled him in a circle. As his legs flew in the air, it occasionally looked as if Mom were going to let go, causing him to fly across the room— yet it never happened. Mom always caught her little son and slowed him to a gentle stop. Years later, the memories of twirling were something the young man thought about often, saying, "What a high level of trust I had in Mom to let her twirl me around the room that way!"

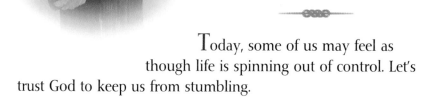

Today, some of us may feel as though life is spinning out of control. Let's trust God to keep us from stumbling.

Be merciful to me,
O God, be merciful to me!
For my soul trusts in You;
And in the shadow of Your wings
I will make my refuge,
Until these calamities have passed by.

PSALM 57:1 NKJV

Guard my life, for I am devoted to you.
You are my God; save your servant
who trusts in you.

PSALM 86:2 NIV

The LORD is my strength and my shield;
in him my heart trusts;
so I am helped, and my heart exults,
and with my song I give thanks to him.

PSALM 28:7 NRSV

You have rescued me from death.
You have kept my feet from stumbling
so that I could walk in your presence,
in the light of life.

PSALM 56:13 GOD'S WORD

The Love of God
Fills Us with Gladness

*Let all those that seek thee rejoice
and be glad in thee: let such as
love thy salvation say continually,
The LORD be magnified.*

PSALM 40:16 KJV

The airplane taxied to the gate, parked, and shut down its engines. Eventually, a steady stream of passengers deplaned and greeted waiting friends and family in the terminal. Tiffany scanned the bustling crowd with an anxious look, looking for her husband. The pilots and flight attendants were the last to leave. Worried, she checked with airline personnel, who informed her that John would be arriving on the next flight. Feelings of relief and joy flooded her heart when she received the news.

Today something may happen to cause us some anxious moments. But we can rejoice in God's constant love and care–no matter what happens.

I will be glad and rejoice in You;
I will sing praise to Your name,
O Most High.

PSALM 9:2 NKJV

Let the righteous rejoice in the LORD
and take refuge in him.
Let all the upright in heart glory.

PSALM 64:10 NRSV

THINK ABOUT GOD'S LOVE
ALL DAY LONG

Oh, how I love your teachings!
They are in my thoughts all day long.

PSALM 119:97 GOD'S WORD

Andrew yawned and tugged on his robe before tiptoeing downstairs. After the pastor's Sunday sermon, he had decided to set the alarm for an hour earlier and start his day by reading God's Word. He opened the Bible at Genesis, but his eyelids slowly closed, and he couldn't stop yawning. Coffee. He scuffed to the kitchen and plugged in the coffee maker, then retrieved the paper from the front yard. By the time he returned to his chair, he realized it was time to get ready for work.

Some of us are morning glories, and others are night owls. Choose the best time of day for you to study. As you fill your mind with God's Word, your heart and spirit will be filled with His love.

The law of his God is in his heart;
None of his steps shall slide.

PSALM 37:31 NKJV

LORD, those you correct are happy;
you teach them from your law.

PSALM 94:12 NCV

Open my eyes to see
the wonderful truths in your law.

PSALM 119:18 NLT

I desire to do your will, O my God;
your law is within my heart.

PSALM 40:8 NIV

God's Love Blots Out
Sins of the Past

Have pity on me, O God, in keeping
with your mercy.
In keeping with your unlimited compassion,
wipe out my rebellious acts.

PSALM 51:1 GOD'S WORD

∽

Every generation has its rebels. Many of us wasted our youths on New Age philosophies and physical desires. When we consider our pasts, we regret those dissipated years. Then Jesus Christ entered our lives, and we turned our backs on rebellion and fell in love with God. But what about our youth? Is it gone forever? In the small book of Joel, God promised to restore what our own selfish behavior stole from us. In God's limitless mercy, He can restore our past and bless us with abundant life.

God's compassion and power are unlimited. Tap into that resource for your needs today.

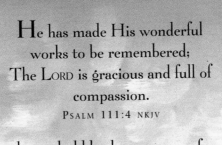

He has made His wonderful
works to be remembered;
The Lord is gracious and full of
compassion.
Psalm 111:4 nkjv

Lord, do not hold back your mercy from me;
let your love and truth always protect me.
Psalm 40:11 ncv

The Lord is good to everyone.
He showers compassion on all his creation.
Psalm 145:9 nlt

As a father has compassion on his children,
so the Lord has compassion on
those who fear him.
Psalm 103:13 niv

THE LOVE OF GOD
RANSOMS FROM DEATH

*He ransoms me from death
and surrounds me with love and
tender mercies.*

PSALM 103:4 NLT

A pickup careened toward Sharon's car as they speeded down the freeway at sixty-five miles per hour. The truck's bumper was mere inches away when the truck swerved back toward the median. Shaking, Sharon pulled to the side of the road and thanked God for His protection and for preserving her life.

While we may not face a near miss on the highway, God already has ransomed our lives from death. Because of His love and tender mercies, we can spend eternity in His presence. Let's celebrate!

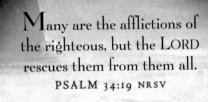

Many are the afflictions of
the righteous, but the LORD
rescues them from them all.

PSALM 34:19 NRSV

He fulfills the desires of those who
reverence and trust him; he hears
their cries for help and rescues them.

PSALM 145:19 TLB

Hear me, O LORD, for Your
lovingkindness is good;
Turn to me according to the
multitude of Your tender mercies.

PSALM 69:16 NKJV

THE LOVE OF GOD IS AWESOME

*For I am constantly aware of your unfailing love,
and I have lived according to your truth.*

PSALM 26:3 NLT

In the middle of a recent morning, Stephen rummaged through his briefcase looking for some paperwork. Instead of what he was looking for, he found a tiny envelope, bearing his name, tucked inside one of the folders. Opening it, he found a few simple but edifying words: "Hope you're having a special day. Can't wait for you to get home." The simple sentiment reminded him of his wife's constant love and affection. Whether together or apart, their love for each other was nurtured in their hearts.

God's Word constantly reminds us of His love, and we can carry His message throughout our day.

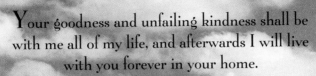

Your goodness and unfailing kindness shall be
with me all of my life, and afterwards I will live
with you forever in your home.

Psalm 23:6 TLB

But the eyes of the Lord are on those who fear him,
on those whose hope is in his unfailing love.

Psalm 33:18 NIV

Your righteousness is an
everlasting righteousness,
and your law is the truth.

Psalm 119:142 NRSV

The Love of God Watches over Us

Truly the eye of the Lord is on those who fear him, on those who hope in his steadfast love.

PSALM 33:18 NRSV

Cheryl's small son bounced in the car with excitement as they headed toward the zoo. At six years old, Phillip loved the

variety of God's creation. As they walked through the Asian Tigers' section, Cheryl took her eyes off her son for only a few moments. When she turned around, he was scrambling past the barrier and toward the tigers' cage. In alarm, she called out to her small son and rescued him from danger.

Whether we are conscious of it or not, God continually watches over us, His children. Because of His care, nothing in our lives happens without His awareness. We can depend on God's steadfast love and attention.

Create in me a clean heart, O God,
And renew a steadfast spirit within me.

PSALM 51:10 NKJV

The fear of the Lord is pure. It endures forever.
The decisions of the Lord are true.
They are completely fair.

PSALM 19:9 GOD'S WORD

Yes, he alone is my Rock, my rescuer,
defense and fortress. Why then should
I be tense with fear when troubles come?

PSALM 62:2 TLB

How great is your goodness
that you have stored up for those who fear you,
that you have given to those who trust you.
You do this for all to see.

PSALM 31:19 NCV

THE LOVE OF GOD FORGIVES SINS
FROM THE PAST

Do not remember the sins
and wrong things I did when I was young.
But remember to love me always
because you are good, LORD.

PSALM 25:7 NCV

A s the students walked into the classroom, the answers for the spelling test were written on the blackboard. After a few minutes of review, the teacher picked up an eraser and wiped

the board clean. When we consider our lives, we have done things we wish could be erased. We carry the painful memory of those mistakes through life, unless we decide to let them go. Our wrongs aren't recorded on a giant blackboard in heaven. If we have confessed our wrongdoing to the Lord and asked for His forgiveness, then God has erased our sins from His memory.

God has already forgiven us. When we come before Him with a contrite heart, He will hear us and never again remember our rebellion. Thank God for His goodness and grace in our lives.

Remember, O LORD, Your tender
mercies and Your lovingkindnesses,
For they are from of old.

PSALM 25:6 NKJV

To such as keep his covenant,
and to those that remember
his commandments to do them.

PSALM 103:18 KJV

But I confess my sins;
I am deeply sorry
for what I have done.

PSALM 38:18 NLT

THE LOVE OF GOD CONQUERS EVIL

You love evil more than good,
Lying rather than speaking righteousness.

PSALM 52:3 NKJV

D ad, everybody is doing it," wheedled Scott. "What's the problem?" Mike recognized the words of peer pressure coming out of his teenager's mouth. His son wanted permission to attend a party where alcohol would be served. The answer was an emphatic no. Often teens, as well as adults, use the worn-out excuse that "everyone is doing it" as a means to give themselves permission to play with evil. *No one will ever see. Why not take that extra deduction on my taxes? Everyone else is doing it.* The all-seeing and all-knowing God sees our actions, whether our fellow man ever catches us at them or not.

Instead of breaking the rules and trying not to get caught, let's focus on getting close to God and His righteousness.

The heavens declare his righteousness;
every nation sees his glory.
PSALM 97:6 NLT

The Lord judges the people of the world.
Judge me, O Lord, according to my righteousness,
according to my integrity.
PSALM 7:8 GOD'S WORD

GOD LOVES THE HONEST

Look at those who are honest and good,
for a wonderful future lies before those
who love peace.

It was only a few weeks after the issuance of the new twenty-dollar bills when Bruce used one in a local grocery store. As the clerk counted the change into his hand, her mistake instantly was apparent. "Whoa, you're giving me too much," he said. She looked surprised. Checking the bill he had handed her, she realized her error; she assumed he had given her a fifty-dollar bill. "Thank you!" she said, smiling. "Not many people would have told me." In fact, many people would have pocketed the extra cash. One opportunity we have to tell others about God is through our daily actions.

As we live in the world with honesty and truth, our lives become a testimony to the people who cross our paths. Make honesty and goodness a part of your actions today.

All goes well for the person who is
generous and lends willingly.
He earns an honest living.
PSALM 112:5 GOD'S WORD

Trust in the LORD, and do good;
so you will live in the land,
and enjoy security.
PSALM 3 7:3 NRSV

You deserve honesty from the heart;
yes, utter sincerity and truthfulness.
Oh, give me this wisdom.
PSALM 51:6 TLB

My hope is in you,
so may goodness and
honesty guard me.
PSALM 25:21 NCV

THE LOVE OF GOD CONTINUES
TO EVERY GENERATION

For the LORD is good;
his steadfast love endures forever,
and his faithfulness to all generations.

PSALM 100:5 NRSV

A whiff of perfume or the scent of an apple pie can catapult us to the past. A turkey roasting might remind us of when we were children and waiting anxiously for Thanksgiving dinner with family. The smell of wood polish brings back memories of a

country church, and the scent of roses often reminds us of a bridal bouquet. Remember the good times . . . the times when God was faithful . . . the times when wet woolen mittens smelled of pine branches gathered for Christmas pageants.

All around us are reminders of God's faithfulness and presence in our lives. Remember His love today.

Praise the LORD.
Give thanks to the LORD, for he is good;
his love endures forever.

Psalm 106:1 NIV

But the mercy of the LORD is
from everlasting to everlasting
upon them that fear him, and his
righteousness unto
children's children;

Psalm 103:17 KJV

THE LOVE OF GOD PROVIDES PEACE

Consider the blameless,
observe the upright;
there is a future
for the man of peace.

PSALM 37:37 NIV

Grandpa Jones's house was a haven of peace. Nothing seemed to bother him. His grandchildren, who lived in the big house up front, regularly slammed in and out of the screen door. They would arrive at dinnertime, when Mom had fixed Dad's favorite liver and onions, or when Grandpa baked his famous oatmeal cookies. Sometimes they would sit on his doorstep crying, needing a hug or a star-spangled adhesive bandage. Grandpa never overreacted; he always listened. Once, his grandson, Joey, asserted, "Grandpa, I think God looks just like you."

Let God's peace rule in your hearts by faith and thanksgiving.

But all who humble themselves before
the Lord shall be given every blessing,
and shall have wonderful peace.

PSALM 37:11 TLB

Great peace have they which love
thy law: and nothing shall offend them.

PSALM 119:165 KJV

For the sake of my family and
friends, I will say,
"Peace be with you."

PSALM 122:8 NLT

GOD'S LOVE SAVES

Make Your face shine upon Your servant;
Save me for Your mercies' sake.

PSALM 31:16 NKJV

On vacation in California for the first time, Theresa and her family spent the day at the beach enjoying the bright sunshine and mild breezes. The next day they looked like red peppers from head to toe, and no amount of aloe vera gel could dim their bright sunburns. It's the same when we spend time with our heavenly Father. While our skin doesn't turn red, we do radiate peace, and our faces glow with the love of God.

Let's spend time with the Lord so His love will shine through our faces. People will notice the difference in our lives.

Restore us, O God;
let your face shine, that we may be saved.

PSALM 80:3 NRSV

On earth people will be loyal to God,
and God's goodness will shine down from heaven.

PSALM 85:11 NCV

The LORD is God,
and he has made his light shine upon us.
With boughs in hand, join in the festal procession
up to the horns of the altar.

PSALM 118:27 NIV

THINK ABOUT GOD'S LOVE

We have thought of thy lovingkindness,
O God, in the midst of thy temple.

PSALM 48:9 KJV

Richard and his six-year-old daughter lay in front of the fireplace, leafing through the family photo album. When he pointed out her grandfather's picture, she asked, "Where does he live?" "In heaven," Richard answered, knowing his father-in-law had loved the Lord with all his heart. Even young children wonder about eternity, and her question gave Richard an opportunity to talk about a world where there are no tears and where the streets are paved with gold. More important, he told her, every moment is spent in the presence of Jesus. The time we spend with God now is only a practice run for eternity.

Every morning, thank God for His eternal love, and throughout your day it will help you keep in mind His long-range plans for you.

Do not withhold Your tender
mercies from me, O LORD;
Let Your lovingkindness and
Your truth continually preserve me.

PSALM 40:11 NKJV

Remember, O LORD, your great mercy and love,
for they are from of old.

PSALM 25:6 NIV

But I trusted in your steadfast love;
my heart shall rejoice in your salvation.

PSALM 13:5 NRSV

The LORD leads with unfailing love
and faithfulness
all those who keep his covenant
and obey his decrees.

PSALM 25:10 NLT

GOD'S LOVE GUIDES US

For His lovingkindness is everlasting.

PSALM 136:14 NAS

Whether Edward was working late in his office or running a Saturday errand at the store, he often glanced down at his wedding ring. To him, the endless circle of gold symbolized the endless love between him and his wife. As he twisted the ring on his finger, it reminded him to celebrate how God had brought them together and blessed them with three wonderful children. It signified a lifetime of smiles, laughter, and sharing. And it reminded him that while his marriage held a special place in his heart, their relationship was even more special because of their mutual love for their heavenly Father.

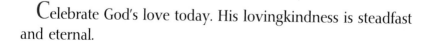

Celebrate God's love today. His lovingkindness is steadfast and eternal.

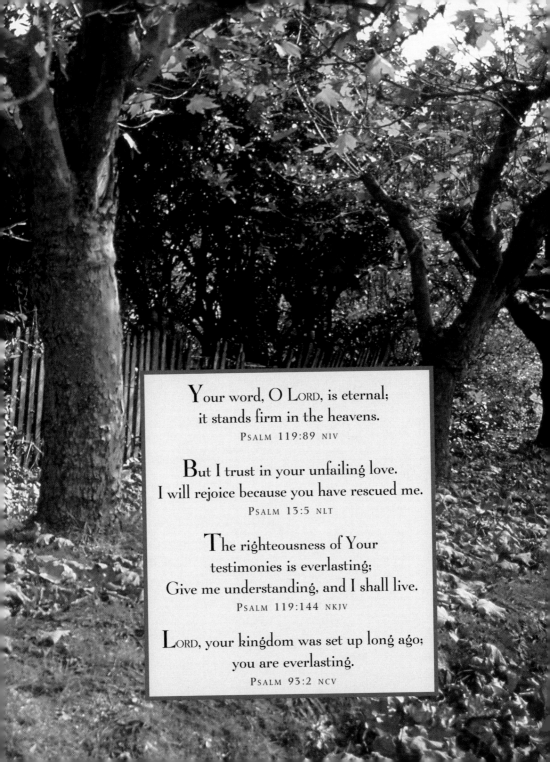

Your word, O Lord, is eternal;
it stands firm in the heavens.
PSALM 119:89 NIV

But I trust in your unfailing love.
I will rejoice because you have rescued me.
PSALM 13:5 NLT

The righteousness of Your
testimonies is everlasting;
Give me understanding, and I shall live.
PSALM 119:144 NKJV

Lord, your kingdom was set up long ago;
you are everlasting.
PSALM 93:2 NCV

THE LOVE OF GOD SHELTERS US

*How precious is Thy
lovingkindness, O God!
And the children of men take refuge in the
shadow of Thy wings.*

PSALM 36:7 NAS

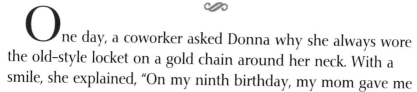

One day, a coworker asked Donna why she always wore the old-style locket on a gold chain around her neck. With a smile, she explained, "On my ninth birthday, my mom gave me

this locket with her photo inside." Donna opened the locket and showed the faded picture. "Mom died several years ago, but this necklace is a constant reminder of her love." We may not have a mental picture of our heavenly Father, but He does give us daily reminders of His presence. The sun's rays gently spreading over the horizon, the soothing sound of a soft rain, and the brilliant colors of nature are all reminders of God's care for us.

Take refuge in God's love today, and let Him remind you of how precious you are to Him.

O my Strength, to you I sing praises,
for you, O God, are my refuge,
the God who shows me unfailing love.

PSALM 59:17 NLT

Protect me as you would protect your own eye.
Hide me under the shadow of your wings.

PSALM 17:8 NCV

O guard my life, and deliver me;
do not let me be put to shame,
for I take refuge in you.

PSALM 25:20 NRSV

TELL OTHERS ABOUT GOD'S LOVE

*I have not kept this Good News
hidden in my heart, but have
proclaimed your lovingkindness
and truth to all the congregation.*

PSALM 40:10 TLB

Matt whistled as he drove the car into the garage and shut off the engine. Earlier in the day, his supervisor had praised him for his work and told him he was getting a year-end bonus and a pay raise. The unexpected announcement was a complete shock! When he opened the door to the kitchen, his wife and kids were in a deep discussion about soccer practice, but he couldn't wait to tell them. He blurted out the good news. "Let's celebrate," his teenage son yelled, and everyone chimed in. "Let's celebrate!"

The ceaseless love and kindness of God are cause for a continual celebration. Tell someone the Good News today.

I raise my voice in praise
and tell of all the miracles you have done.

PSALM 26:7 NCV

That I may proclaim with
the voice of thanksgiving
And declare all Thy wonders.

PSALM 26:7 NAS

The heavens declare the glory of God,
and the sky displays
what his hands have made.

PSALM 19:1 GOD'S WORD

Sing to the LORD, bless His name;
Proclaim the good news of His
salvation from day to day.

PSALM 96:2 NKJV

GREAT IS GOD'S LOVE

But may all who seek you rejoice
and be glad in you;
may those who love your salvation always say,
"The Lord be exalted!"

PSALM 40:16 NIV

For hours Maggie sat in the wallpaper store and flipped through stacks of sample books. Occasionally she would pause and study a particular pattern, then shake her head saying, "No, that's not the one." The clerks were impressed by her determination. In her mind's eye Maggie could see the perfect wallpaper, and so she continued searching. Eventually she found the pattern—one from her own childhood. "It's just what we need for our first baby's room," she explained. If she had been scouring the floor for a lost diamond earring, she would have been no more diligent. God longs for us to be as diligent in spiritual matters.

When we finally acknowledge our relationship with our heavenly Father and regularly seek to grow in our understanding of Him, He rejoices. Let's continue with all diligence to grow in our relationship with God.

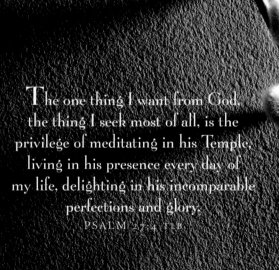

The one thing I want from God,
the thing I seek most of all, is the
privilege of meditating in his Temple,
living in his presence every day of
my life, delighting in his incomparable
perfections and glory.

PSALM 27:4 TLB

THE LOVE OF GOD IS MY REFUGE

But I will sing of Your power;
Yes, I will sing aloud of Your
mercy in the morning;
For You have been my defense
And refuge in the day of my trouble.

PSALM 59:16 NKJV

∞

The doors of the bathroom slammed from time to time. Downstairs, Connie wondered what on earth her eighteen-year-old son was doing. Eventually he thundered down the stairs with a couple of overflowing cardboard boxes. "Where are you going?" she asked. "Kevin got his own place, and I'm moving in with him," he said, avoiding her eyes. "I thought you were going to live at home and save enough for college." Even though she tried to dissuade him, Connie finally let her son go, praying that God would take care of him. Sometimes people disappoint us, but we can't control their actions. However, we can depend on our relationship with God. He has our best interests at heart.

❧

God is our refuge when sadness threatens to overwhelm us. He is our defense in the day of trouble.

For you are my hiding place;
you protect me from trouble.
You surround me with songs of victory.

PSALM 32:7 NLT

Guard my soul and deliver me;
Do not let me be ashamed,
for I take refuge in Thee.

PSALM 25:20 NAS

THE LOVE OF GOD CONTINUES FOREVER

For the Lord is always good.
He is always loving and kind,
and his faithfulness goes on and
on to each succeeding generation.

PSALM 100:5 TLB

❧

When Roberta looked out her bedroom window, the nearby Rocky Mountains were veiled in a hazy, gray mist. The dark clouds threatened rain, and moments later, with a crack of thunder, the sky opened up. After several hours of a steady downpour, the rain stopped, and, through a crack in the eastern sky, rays of sunlight streamed down, creating a brilliant, arching rainbow. Then as quickly as they rolled in, the clouds disappeared and were replaced with bright sunshine and deep blue skies. Both rain and sunshine fall in our daily lives. It's the same with our emotions: Sometimes we're happy, and sometimes we're sad. We need consistency in our lives, which only comes from the eternal God. He is always good, loving, and kind.

From generation to generation, we can count on God's faithfulness. Let's celebrate the goodness and consistency of God's love in our lives.

Trust the Lord, and do good things.
Live in the land, and practice being faithful.

PSALM 37:3 GOD'S WORD

O love the LORD, all you
His godly ones!
The LORD preserves the faithful
And fully recompenses the proud doer.

PSALM 31:2 3 NAS

O taste and see that the LORD is good;
happy are those who take refuge in him.

PSALM 34:8 NRSV

THE LOVE OF GOD IS MY STRENGTH

*For your unfailing love is as high
as the heavens.
Your faithfulness reaches to the clouds.*

PSALM 57:10 NLT

Ruth slipped quickly under the heavy down comforter and cuddled next to her sleeping husband, careful not to wake him. As she drifted off to a peaceful sleep, she found his presence comforting. The touch of a hand or a gentle hug provides reassurance. Whether we are married or single, God surrounds us with His loving arms and covers us with His presence.

Thank God for His unfailing love and eternal faithfulness.

I have not hidden Your righteousness
within my heart;
I have declared Your faithfulness and
Your salvation;
I have not concealed Your lovingkindness and
Your truth
From the great assembly.
PSALM 40:10 NKJV

GOD'S LOVE AND FAITHFULNESS
REACH THE CLOUDS

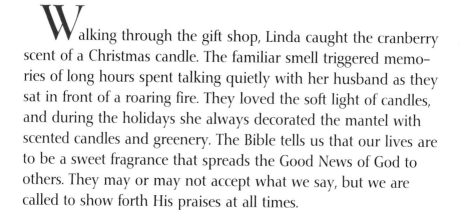

My God in His lovingkindness
will meet me;
God will let me look
triumphantly upon my foes.

PSALM 59:10 NAS

Walking through the gift shop, Linda caught the cranberry scent of a Christmas candle. The familiar smell triggered memories of long hours spent talking quietly with her husband as they sat in front of a roaring fire. They loved the soft light of candles, and during the holidays she always decorated the mantel with scented candles and greenery. The Bible tells us that our lives are to be a sweet fragrance that spreads the Good News of God to others. They may or may not accept what we say, but we are called to show forth His praises at all times.

As we live faithfully in God's love, the Lord lives through us.

But I trust in your unfailing love;
my heart rejoices in your salvation.
PSALM 13:5 NIV

For Your lovingkindness is before my eyes,
And I have walked in Your truth.
PSALM 26:3 NKJV

His anger lasts only a moment,
but his kindness lasts for a lifetime.
Crying may last for a night,
but joy comes in the morning.
PSALM 30:5 NCV

Your kindness and love are as vast
as the heavens. Your faithfulness
is higher than the skies.
PSALM 57:10 TLB

THE LOVE OF GOD SUPPORTS ME

If I say, "My foot slips,"
Your mercy, O Lord, will hold me up.

PSALM 94:18 NKJV

Lost, Jack kept driving, certain that around the next bend he and his wife would come to a familiar landmark on the map. It never came, and eventually he had to swallow his pride and ask for directions. Instead of arriving at his sister's wedding on time, they had to slip into a back pew during the service. When our feet stumble and we step off the right path, it's important to ask for God's help and mercy.

The Lord never meant for us to find our own way through life. He is ready to show us the way; all we need to do is ask Him for directions.

Do not, O LORD, withhold
your mercy from me;
let your steadfast love and your faithfulness
keep me safe forever.

PSALM 40:11 NRSV

Certainly, goodness and mercy will stay close
to me all the days of my life,
and I will remain in the Lord's house for
days without end.

PSALM 23:6 GOD'S WORD

But I am like a sheltered olive tree
protected by the Lord himself. I trust
in the mercy of God forever and ever.

PSALM 52:8 TLB

I cry out to the LORD;
I plead for the LORD's mercy.

PSALM 142:1 NLT

THE LOVE OF GOD NEVER ENDS

My mercy will stay with him forever.
My promise to him is unbreakable.

PSALM 89:28 GOD'S WORD

"**B**ut you promised," Jimmy cried into the phone, although he knew it wasn't his dad's fault that he couldn't make it home in time for his birthday. An unexpected blizzard had closed down the Chicago airport, and it would be morning before the runways were cleared. Still, he wanted to blame somebody for his disappointment. Despite our best intentions, we all break promises—to our children, to our friends, to ourselves. Cars break down, airplanes are rerouted, people make mistakes. But a broken promise still hurts. God in His infinite mercy has given us an unbreakable promise. His mercy endures forever.

God keeps His promises. Let's work at keeping ours.

The Lord's promise is sure. He speaks
no careless word; all he says is purest
truth, like silver seven times refined.

PSALM 12:6 TLB

When I suffer, this comforts me:
Your promise gives me life.

PSALM 119:50 NCV

He is the one who made heaven and earth,
the sea, and everything in them.
He is the one who keeps every promise forever.

PSALM 146:6 NLT

Surely goodness and lovingkindness will
follow me all the days of my life,
And I will dwell in the house of the LORD forever.

PSALM 23:6 NAS

THE LOVE OF GOD IS SAFE

Because your steadfast love
is better than life,
my lips will praise you.

PSALM 63:3 NRSV

After scrubbing up, Floyd walked into the neonatal unit and looked down at his fragile son, who had been born a few hours earlier. Floyd Jr. was three months premature and weighed only slightly more than two pounds. Wires and tubes almost hid his tiny body. The doctor made no promises that the baby would live. Floyd prayed fervently for his son's life and placed him in God's hands. Whether we live many years or only a few hours, in the scope of eternity all our journeys here are short. Yet our relationship with the Lord of the universe and His love are eternal.

Celebrate the steadfast love of God, which is better than life

Create in me a pure heart, O God,
and renew a steadfast spirit within me.

PSALM 51:10 NIV

He will not fear evil tidings;
His heart is steadfast,
trusting in the LORD.

PSALM 112:7 NAS

Pour out your unfailing love
on those who know you!
Never stop giving your
salvation to those who
long to do your will.

PSALM 36:10 TLB

THE LOVE OF GOD CAUSES HOPE TO RISE

For my love they are my adversaries:
but I give myself unto prayer.

PSALM 109:4 KJV

Jason met his sleepy sister, Janet, at the coffee shop on the corner of the campus. "You look like you haven't slept in a week," he said, laughing. "What's up?" Janet proceeded to tell her brother about her problem roommate, her best friend from high school, who seemed to be more interested in partying all night than in studying. "If this keeps up, I'll never pass my eight o'clock biology class." Jason's advice seemed too simple: Find another roommate. Janet finally admitted that her friendship was jeopardizing her grades.

Human relationships come and go, yet our spiritual relationship with God continues. It's a solid rock of hope.

The LORD will command
His lovingkindness in the daytime;
And His song will be with me in the night,
A prayer to the God of my life.

PSALM 42:8 NAS

The LORD has heard my supplication;
The LORD will receive my prayer.

PSALM 6:9 NKJV

Listen to my prayer for mercy
as I cry out to you for help,
as I lift my hands toward your holy sanctuary.

PSALM 28:2 NLT

THE LOVE OF GOD
IS WORTH MORE THAN LIFE

Love and truth belong to God's people;
goodness and peace will be theirs.

PSALM 85:10 NCV

Long-term marriages are built on love, trust, and truth. They are a three-strand cord that is not easily broken, consisting of a husband, a wife, and Christ. Peace eludes some couples because their relationships are not built on a solid, spiritual foundation. When a couple makes peace with themselves and with God, they will find peace in their homes.

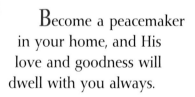

Become a peacemaker in your home, and His love and goodness will dwell with you always.

He hath delivered my soul in peace
from the battle that was against me:
for there were many with me.
PSALM 55:18 KJV

Those who love your law have great peace
and do not stumble.
PSALM 119:165 NLT

I will both lie down and sleep in peace;
for you alone, O LORD, make
me lie down in safety.
PSALM 4:8 NRSV

But all who humble themselves before
the Lord shall be given every blessing,
and shall have wonderful peace.
PSALM 37:11 TLB

GOD'S LOVE IS CHANGELESS

My God is changeless in his love
for me and he will come and help
me. He will let me see my wish
come true upon my enemies.

PSALM 59:10 TLB

The two boys stood toe to toe on the dusty baseball diamond, each stubbornly refusing to give way. "You're out!" yelled one ten-year-old. "It was a ball!" the other one shouted back. Just then the coach put his arms around both of them as they glared at each other. "Come on, guys," he said calmly. "It's only a ball game." When we have a difference of opinion, we all win when we're willing to change and compromise. While it's a human characteristic to compromise, and necessary for our growth, we rejoice in the changeless nature of God. His love and compassion for us never waver.

God is steadfast in His love and concern for us. While our relationships may change, we celebrate His unchanging love.

Create in me a pure heart, O God,
and renew a steadfast spirit within me.

PSALM 51:10 NIV

Surely goodness and lovingkindness will
follow me all the days of my life,
And I will dwell in the house of the LORD forever.

PSALM 23:6 NAS

God's Love
Is Worth More than Gold

Therefore I love Your commandments
More than gold, yes, than fine gold!

PSALM 119:127 NKJV

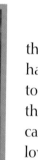

The card was tucked between the pages of an old Bible Sarah hadn't used in a while. When she took it off the shelf and flipped through it, an old anniversary card fell out. It began, "To my loving husband. . . ." Memories of that night flooded her mind: It was their fifth anniversary and the first time they could afford dinner at a nice restaurant. Their financial circumstances had improved through the years, and their love had grown deeper. God's love for us is as deep as the ocean and as fresh as His first word to us. The Bible is a love letter from God.

Hold on to God's eternal promises and spend some time reading His love letter to you.

A for God, his way is perfect.
All the LORD's promises prove true.
He is a shield for all who look to him for protection.
PSALM 18:30 NLT

Make me walk in the path of Thy commandments,
For I delight in it.
PSALM 119:35 NAS

He will keep his agreement forever;
he will keep his promises always.
PSALM 105:8 NCV

THE LOVE OF GOD SATISFIES

*Satisfy us in the morning with your unfailing love,
so we may sing for joy to the end of our lives.*

PSALM 90:14 NLT

What is the secret of true happiness? Some people search for it through a relationship or in some achievement. Everyone

seems to be searching for ultimate fulfillment and happiness, but few people find it. The truth is, when we touch others with a sincere love, it satisfies our quest for happiness. Reaching out to others with Christlike love brings true joy.

While we cherish our relationship with a spouse or special friend, we prize our relationship with our heavenly Father. His unfailing love satisfies us and fills our life with joy.

You will show me the path of life;
In Your presence is fullness of joy;
At Your right hand are pleasures
forevermore.

PSALM 16:11 NKJV

THE FAITHFUL HISTORY OF GOD'S LOVE

Whoever is wise
will remember these things
and will think about the love
of the Lord.

PSALM 107:43 NCV

No one enjoys the trials of life, but in the midst of them, we face an important choice. Either we plunge into negative emotions, or we see these tests as a search for some positive aspect in a situation. Instead of bemoaning circumstances, praise God for His unfailing love and faithfulness. God's Word tells us it is wise to turn our attention to our Lord and focus on His love, even when we are faced with adversity.

The wise focus on God's lessons of love in every situation—positive or negative.

Teach us to number our days aright,
that we may gain a heart of wisdom.

PSALM 90:12 NIV

The LORD looks down from heaven on humankind
to see if there are any who are wise,
who seek after God.

PSALM 14:2 NRSV

The fear of the LORD is the beginning of wisdom;
A good understanding have all those who do
His commandments;
His praise endures forever.

PSALM 111:10 NAS

Honor and Love God's Commands

*I lift my hands in prayer because of
your commandments, which I love.
I will reflect on your laws.*

PSALM 119:48 GOD'S WORD

For many people, prayer is formal and confined to the inside of the church. To Gary, talking with the Lord is as natural as breathing. In every situation, whether saying a blessing in a fast-food restaurant or visiting a sick friend, Gary utters the words, *Let's pray*, then sends up an appropriate prayer. As we increase our awareness of the eternal and always-present God, we learn He is a constant friend who wants to be involved in every aspect of our lives.

Prayer–whether long or short–is vital to a loving relationship with God. Let's purpose to talk to Him as we would a friend, and to love Him more with each passing day.

Yet day by day the Lord also pours
out his steadfast love upon me, and
through the night I sing his songs
and pray to God who gives me life.

PSALM 42:8 TLB

The Lord shows his true love every day.
At night I have a song,
and I pray to my living God.

PSALM 42:8 NCV

O You who hear prayer,
To You all men come.

PSALM 65:2 NAS

Praise be to God,
who has not rejected my prayer
or withheld his love from me!

PSALM 66:20 NIV

This and other books in the Psalms Gift Edition™ series are available from your local bookstore.

Lighthouse Psalms

Garden Psalms

Love Psalms

If you have enjoyed this book, or if it has impacted your life, we would like to hear from you. Please contact us at:

Honor Books
Department E
P.O. Box 55388
Tulsa, Oklahoma 74155

Or by e-mail at info@honorbooks.com